A Parallel World

A PARALLEL WORLD
AN ANTHOLOGY OF POETRY
BY ROXANA

INSPIRATION

Kudos to the two great poets of our time – Rumi & Kabir. These two great minds have enabled an introspection of self; and reflection on the gifts ordained by He who is above all else. They have inspired the author to pen her thoughts in her poetic treasures.

"Nothing is mine, within myself
Whatever there is, is Yours O Lord
If I surrender to You, what is already Yours
I lose nothing, only gain your pleasure."

Kabir, 15th-century Indian mystic poet and saint.

"Let the waters settle;
And you will see the moon and the stars
mirrored in your own being."

Rumi, 13th-century Persian poet and Islamic scholar.

NOTE TO THE READER

Poems contained in this short labour of love deals with my life experiences and the lessons gleaned from them. These poems which are categorized in the genres of Ode, Allegory, Epic, and Soliloquy is an exploration of spirituality and philosophy.

The meaning will come alive if the poems are read aloud and in a slow tempo. I have had several poetic soirees: both live (with a few people, following COVID 19 restrictions of social distancing) and zoom webinars. My poem, 'Well I Never' was accepted with great acclaim at a sustainability award ceremony where I presented it as part of the acceptance speech. I find the poem to be relatable as we all went through the lockdown earlier on with trepidation.

The words of the poems are enough on their own; however, I have had the blessing of being associated with such marvellous artists that I felt it important for them to give a visual rendition to my words. The ethos of each poem has been beautifully visualised in their creative work, and to each I say, you are creative geniuses. Thank you for participating in my poetic journey, literally. I am honoured to know each of you ladies as you hail from different parts of the world, it truly affirms my conviction on the collective potential that diversity brings.

THIS BOOK IS LOVINGLY DEDICATED TO MY ALMA MATER.

My Mother who adopted me and showered me with greater love than her own children she gave birth to after my adoption.

The poem 'My Mater' describes her love and dedication which made her the beautiful person she was inside and out, and which was written seven months before she passed.

May you rest in peace

ACKNOWLEDGEMENTS

I want to start with an utmost thanks to my husband, Sadru-din Jaffer. He has been my anchor through and through and especially when he painstakingly listened to my non-stop ranting as I put the content together for this book.

My sisters, Deenaz & Shahina, who patiently listened to my poetry and who helped me with their valuable feedback.

My friends, especially Kusum Dutta, with whom I am connected on the same spiritual plane.

All the talented artists who gave me such beautiful visual renditions of my poems that they completely resounded with the ethos of my work.

Firoze Edassery, who helped me in the compilation of my poems along with its graphics. Thank you so much for the meaningful graphic covers.

And finally, God, whose attributes I am eternally in awe of, and who gave me an opportunity to reflect and understand his magnitude and magnanimity.

TABLE OF CONTENTS

MY MATER

Not from your womb, but from your veins
Your blood pumps into me, in every which way
Teacher, influencer, indeed my inspiration
Giver at each step, at each action, my motivation

........Indeed, a role model this Alma Mater

Trend Breaker, before your times
India, to Kenya to UK, in the 50's
In pursuit of the degree, to help the children of the lesser kind
Be they deaf, dumb, autistic or blind

..... Indeed, a role model this Alma Mater

Legacy Leaver, Barnet Asian Women's drop-in centre lives on
Understanding the depressed and the oppressed to go on
Aiding them to be counted, as the Ministry gets impressed
Accolading this Asian lady in the midst of the elite and the noblest

..... Indeed, a role model this Alma Mater

Not from your womb, but definitely of the same rib
Waking up in the wee hours to check if I'm still in the crib
Nursing my accidents and falls from the roof selflessly
Saffron milk with lessons of love about humanity

..... Indeed, a role model this Alma Mater

Helpless today, in a hospital bed, lays this lady
Still caring, still giving, with nothing to give
Purring, hardly audible, advising to look after others in pain
Not complaining of the pain that is only lessened with morphine

..... Indeed, a role model this Alma Mater

Helpless I am, as distance separates us, far - yet so near,
Can't repay those endless caresses, those words of encouragement
Can't wipe those tears of solitude or kiss those rosy cheeks
Please God, Help my Mater, as all she wants is to rest in her finery that once was.

..... Indeed, a role model this Alma Mater

Poem - My Mater
Artist's Depiction: *'Hope'*
By Afshan Quraishy - India

DEVOTION THROUGH DHIKR

Heart in a pulsating mode; in rhythm with the breath
Mind reaching its zenith; as thoughts meet their death

Gratefulness taking over; conveying lightness to the body
Entire body in smiles; perhaps the spiritual light in embody

All because of the Dhikr; the constant chanting
His attributes in tempo, energy in sync; all else negating

Dhikr
What an effect on the waves of the Gamma and the Theta
Both leave defeated, allowing the take-over by the wave of relaxing Alpha

Dhikr
Bringing an awareness of His elements; so many… Ninety-nine
An inner need arises; to ascribe, to impute these traits divine

Dhikr
My heart is in a pulsating mode, in sync with the mind
Now there is total unity; as mind, body and soul are totally entwined.

Poem - Devotion Through Dhikr
Artist's Depiction: *'Together'*
By Majo Portillo - Netherlands

MAYA

Shhh Listen to the quiet; Ti's loud
Soundlessness is enticing, Ti's inviting
Boarding the flight, internal and inbound
Letting go, indeed a secretive flitting

       Inner recesses to the inner realms
       Beyond the veil of illusion
       Into the abyss of the Anselms
       Out with abusion, out with confusion

Neither we, nor I, neither you, nor me
No what, and why, no here or there
Riding up the waterfall with glee
Up and up the colourless stair

       Sixth sense now beyond certainty
       Chakra of the Third Eye intuitive
       Past Maya to blissful Eternity
       Inbound Flight totally lucrative

So lucrative; Shhh Listen to the quiet; Ti's loud

Poem - Maya
Artist's Depiction: *'Utopia'*
By Minisha Bharadwaj - India

THE SCORNED SHE
Dedicated to the Spurned Female Heroes

Green Gables Anne, with sheer disbelief, exclaimed
"A Rose is fragrant only by its name,
Not as a thistle or a skunk cabbage, Labelled?"
Ti's beauty marred, Ti's strength lamed

Insecurities, disquiet of the self, come to rise
As women label their own sex
Jealousy, resent, envy, just to sensationalize
'More deadly than a male' is she when in deflex

Labels are for control, but only the labeller is reduced
Definitions belong to the definers, not the defined
A laughing stock, pigeonholed to make you look better
Only negates the labelled, getting you close to the abettor

Na Green Gables Anne, you are wrong
A rose labelled by any name
Is still beautiful with its fragrance
Ti's beauty not marred nor strength lamed.

Poem - The Scorned She
Artist's Depiction: *'Madonna'*
By Sonal Purohit - India

REALIZATION QUINTAIN

With unflinching faith
Stand I, with my head bowed
Walking, path of righteousness is my aim
Refraining from evil avowed
So I may depart fulfilled and proud.

Comes the time when one errs
Allows a mistake of another
As being unreported affairs
Allowing the crime to further
As if not my crime but of the other

With reflection is realization
Protection is uninformed and blind
There is no parallelization
Rules for abetting are defined
Just as light of peace is designed

The world is engulfed in darkness
The light of happiness is diminishing
The human becoming frail in this harshness
Standing short with a million shortcoming
Believing in the power that is forgiving

O Lord, hold me firm as I ask
Reply with kindness for my evil
Such is the strength under your mask
Omnipotent are thee primeval
That, even a moonless night grows regal

You who stands tall, is forgiving
The world exists due to your benevolence
May every step of mine be of loving
May every action and thought be in reverence
As I prostate to thee without arrogance

Poem – Realization Quintain
Artist's Depiction: *'Naissance'*
By Sneh Mehta – UK

SHE SILLY SALLY

She silly Sally sitting on the sea shore
    She silly Sally sees a sea gull high above

Silly Sally wondering wherefore bound the gull?
    Solo and sure, free n so convinced, strong n so sure
Solo n unique, yet high and liberated
    High, Higher, Highest the bird nearly blurred
As Silly Sally remains counting shells, first second third....

Silly Sally now reflective, counting shells totally pensive
    Walks to the sea, with no a care, flapping her arms, being ostensive
Why sell shells on the beach, when I can go up and reach
    The bird; No the clouds; No the sky; No beyond what I can't see,
I must, I have to get there, I have to go beyond, and I may find Me

Yes I will be me, not Silly Sally, but the angel that I'm meant to be
    I can fly, high, higher, highest, I have wings, I don't need shells to hold Me down
I have wings that hold me up that will take Me beyond me, to the light
    I will find the source, up above that makes my shells shimmer and bright
There is no stopping me Sally; I'm truly that angel in flight

No more Silly, Sally, on the sea shore
    But an Angel Above, Happy, that Sally saw the sea gull above.
Unstoppable; flapping her arms- not her wings; being ostensive.
    Silly Sally? Indeed not any more.
Sally, fully actualized, her potential realized, she is silly no more.

Poem - She Silly Sally
Artist's Depiction: *'Pearls'*
By Kusum Dutta - India

BEYOND SHOONYA

My mind; my sanctuary.
Emitting deep thoughts;
Carving a sculpture of words,
Reaching lofty heights.
Yes. My mind: The Esoteric sanctuary of my exoteric being

Pain, Needs, Wants, Disappearing
Love, Warmth, Nothing, Appearing
Back, Back, Back… till Shoonya
Nothingness, nothingness, limitless
Yes. My Mind: My sanctuary.

Non-doing, distancing, engaging, anchoring
Stillness to happiness; unbound ecstasy
Past consciousness nothing of me
Only bliss and exultation; only bliss without me
Yes. My Mind: My sanctuary.

My Mind: The esoteric sanctuary of my exoteric being
Nothing Left to report, Only Peace, Peace and more Peace
Yes, My mind: my sanctuary.

Poem - Shoonya
Artist's Depiction: '*The Search*'
By Kusum Dutta - India

STUD IN THE MUD

Eyes glossy and watery
Teeth without an apple bite;
Hair sparse and silvery
As if a man on his last flight

Pulled to the mirror in fright
Behold the once upon a time stud;
Wrinkles and chins; yet still alight
Not quite ready to hit the mud

Must have a sight of a fair damsel
For that fast heartbeat and stirring;
Professing undying love for an angel
Eureka grey cells alert with a buzzing

Face and carcass now worn, yet heart childlike;
Body time short, yet ready for that nothingness spike.

Poem - Stud in the Mud
Artist's Depiction: *'Reverie'*
By Minisha Bharadwaj - India

THE ULTIMATE DESIGN

Wherefore is the Artist, the Creator and The Architect of this Ultimate Design?
Pause, think, marvel, and reflect on its being;
Award less, without Cheer, nor any Appreciation, glory taken as if all mine
Revel in the design; change NOW the unseeing to the seeing

Travel inside to the labyrinth of the Ultimate
Explore the rhythm, of the 100,000 daily beats;
Hear every day, the 2000 gallons being intimate
Within the hearts road network in its untiring feats

Still in the inner, listen to the lungs, as they take my breath away
17,000 gulps of air taken per day, unnoticed and unseen;
Marvel at the gut, in its second by second alkaline affray
Neutralizing the stomach acid in its effort to keep it clean

50,000 daily thoughts equalling to 35 per second passing freely
In a busy untiring uncomplaining brain;
And 28,000 ten-second blinks, actioned discreetly
Indeed a voluntary reflex for the visual fast lane

Wake up dear, reflect on the unmentioned: the hair, the skin, the cells,
Be they red, white or skin. Do not forget the saliva and the sperm;
Reflect on the kidney, the liver and reproductive parallels
So who is the architect of this ultimate design of our term?

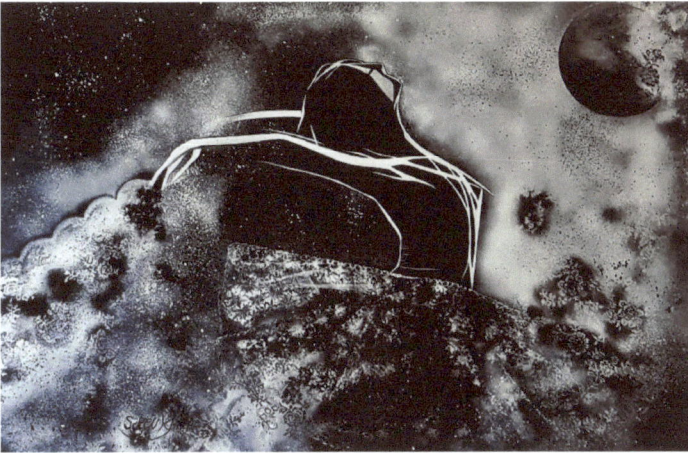

Poem – The Ultimate Design
Artist's Depiction: *'Refugee Dream'*
By Seren Khalaf - Syria

WAVES

Waves
   Bewildering
     Unstoppable
       Enveloping
         Dramatic in its natural cascade
           Waves
             Continuous Secretive
             Forceful
             Unafraid, on its own crusade
           Waves
             A force of its own
             Growing ferocious
           Drowning with its might; not
         Afraid of its flight
       A mountain of water as if an
     Angry sea monster
   Waves
     Wherefore bound?
   Unitedly Individual
 Rhythmic in its journey, a one many army
Lapping the ground, as if homebound
Waves
Purring, reach its ebb
 A wordless voice, returning by choice
   Ego totally dusted, path of the Origin lusted
     No more now, indeed is much more now
       Waves
            Ti's a movement between the shores of our soul

Poem - Waves
Artist's Depiction: *'Musical Ripple'*
By Sonal Purohit - India

WELL I NEVER...

Well I Never...

COVID 19, you came to destruct,
    And Lockdown 20, you came to obstruct
Order of the day: "Stay at home"
    An opportunity to relax n catch up with sleep
Or a chance to question His existence deep
    No resistance now in the discovery of AUM?
AUM the sacred sound of the universe
    Found in every nook and cranny like a poetic verse

Well I Never...

To the garden perambulating the home
    Round and Round; looking for the Unknown
As Adam found Eve in His Garden of Eden
    Many jewels in my garden; blatant to my Oblivion
All speaking in colour and shape, flower bush and tree
    Iqra — Read, Read what you know not, come set yourself free
Learn the sound of AUM through the birds of the sky
    Recite with the mind; find the power of the butterfly

Well I Never...

AUM exists; in the many shades of red and pink
    Juxtaposed with variegated greens all in sync
Green berries flowering to pink; Honey bees in search of nectar
    Confused with beautiful butterflies on their path as protector
Cant but just appreciate what I never saw before
    Blessings manifold of the birds in their original couture
The Neem, the Lime, the Chikoo & Moringa opening their boughs
    Guests invited to perch are the parrot, the dove and the crows

Well I Never...

Look everywhere and there is diversity in total harmony
    Not castles in the air, but the moon dancing round the planets
Under the moonlight am I, a whirling dervish on the lawn
    Moving to the rhythm of AUM not aware when night becomes dawn
Twirling in happiness becoming submerged in His current
    He who is above all else, only His cell is totally apparent
COVID 19, did you really come to destruct?
    Really you helped to right the wrongs and reconstruct

Poem - Well I Never
Artist's Depiction: *'As Samad'*
By Sumaira Isaacs - Pakistan

WHY O WHY

Why O Why, Can't I hear the rain speak?
That's the chat-up line of the tall shiny green blade of grass As he bowed down to the cerise pink rose in a deep caress
The proud rose, averting, turned her full body of petals, to her love, the yellow Sun-flower.
Lest there be a pang of jealousy? But as usual nonchalant; as if not now; not this hour
Peering for his life-line up in the sky, beseeching the red ball of fire to peep over the teary cloud
The red sun-like tomato under him, faithful to the tee, turned his netting towards the large daisy
"Shh quiet, let's relax under the tears" cried the indigo and violet delphis being totally lazy
"Seize the moment; enjoy the grey for a brighter tomorrow;" whimpers the plum aubergine

Why O Why, Can't I hear the rain speak?
Disappointed, the shiny green blade of grass now turns to the Bird of Paradise
Regal he is with his orange and blue petals standing in magnificence
With a good perspective on life, declares "See how I stand, looking like a bird in flight"
Counsels: "seek for knowledge of this beautiful spectrum of nature; reflect and stand upright"
"Find a guide, find a guru, and soothe your anxiety. Ask the rain…….."

Why O Why, Can't I hear the rain speak?
Cries the tall shiny green blade of grass
Guru, wherefore art thou? The Multi-coloured butterfly? Disdain as he stops flower to flower.
Perhaps this pearly bubble of air trapped in the rain, translucent yet with colours of the hour
Check his flight — wherefore headed this beautiful bubble? PHATT, bursting at his seams
And revealing From edge to edge; all colours together; aah The Real Spectrum
From Left to Right; Violet, Indigo, Blue, Green, Yellow, Orange and Red; the Real Centrum
Search is over, green grass reflecting, seeing himself, not divided, only united like a rainbow

Poem - Why O Why
Artist's Depiction: *'Whimsical'*
By Zaahirah Muthy - Mauritius

SARI PALLU

A piece of fabric 6 yards long,
One yard left trailing of this sarong
Body draped to hide the sensuous self
Over the left shoulder of myself

Elegant this one yard trail
With uses much more of this veil
Whether for drying children's tears
Or as a hand towel for the dirty ears

Providing an anchor for the shy kids
Or becoming a cover for the sleepy eyelids
Remover of hot pans from the stove
Emitting a fragrance of a winter clove

Is this useful Pallu, just a very long yard
A giver of warmth, or a useful arm guard
A carrier of sweet scented flowers and scattered toys
A purposeful piece of fabric ready to poise

Best of all drawing a simile to the Supreme
A giver of love, warmth, fragrance and esteem
A drape for the sensuous self indeed
But uses of a protector decreed.

Poem - Sari Pallu
Artist's Depiction: *'Sylph'*
By Afshan Quraishy - India

PEEK-A-BOO

I'm the follicle held with the chord
Swimming up to see the world
      Whilst blinded by the noise
      Am real excited by the Voice

Must be Mater? Or is it Pater?
Arrival has to be postponed to later
      Don't want to shatter the peace
      And bring in the unease.

Let me swim some more
Let me be 'me' for some more
      The chord is my lifeline
      With it I'm upbeat and sanguine

Am grown now, no more a follicle
A body still attached like a Popsicle
      Enjoying my space but a little lonely
      Feeling warm but not homely

Have solitude yet want to know Moo n Poo
Can I? Just take one Peek-a-boo?
      Oops, curiosity killed the cat
      Out of the door and in the net

O dear, Whoosh down the hatch
Fast with the mulch and the mash
      Is poor me, a follicle that was at rest
      Now a young chap nuzzled her breast

Ti's not the same, not upbeat and sanguine.
Want to return to my lifeline
      But this a ticket of NO return
Have to pass the test, and then turn

What have I done? Oh, what have I done?
A Peek-a-boo that cannot be undone
      Pay the penance, go and live
      Arrive. Behave. Connive. Contrive

From peace of strife, is this the lesson of life?
Seek the Giver of peace, the giver of tranquillity
      That was before Peek-a -Boo, which was me
      Now I know, He is Me and Me is He

So let me be, let me try and find He
So I can be that follicle without the Peek-a-Boo

Poem - Peek a Boo
Artist's Depiction: *'Windows of the Soul'*
By Graciela Ghirardosi - Argentina

A PARALLEL WORLD
THE ANTHOLOGY'S GIST

Each route I go, each place I arrive at, opens new doors
Each opened doors leads me to newer adventures

Big fires burn in my heart, crazy horses ride within my soul,
Tell me what is at the end of this melee

Why is there such a painful stupor?

Or is it calmness with the vague images of the saviour and sages
Why do these servants of You meet with me ⊠ a mere mortal?
There has to be a reason for sure

Dear God do not leave me to my desires

They only result in short-lived tranquillity
Meet me with all your servants

Explain the mysteries, help this non-observant
Show me the signs of The Parallel World

The World that is of bliss with mercy all swirled.

Poem - A Parallel World
Artist's Depiction: *'Al-Ahad (The One)'*
By Sumaira Isaacs – Pakistan

GLOSSARY OF TERMS

Al-Ahad (Arabic): The One

Anselms: Saints

As-Samad (Arabic): The ever Lasting

Aum (Sanskrit): Cosmic power behind all creation

Chakra: Spinning energy points in the body

Chikoo: An evergreen tree bearing edible fruit with Sweet yellow-brown flesh.

Dhikr (Arabic): Remembrance by repeating God's name

Iqra: Means "read!" The first command sent down by Allah to Prophet Mohammed (PBUH) through the angel Gabriel deemed as the first word of the Qur'an

Maya (Sanskrit): Illusion

Neem: A tall, tropical evergreen tree of the mahogany Family, cultivated for its aromatic oil.

Pallu: The Loose end of a Sari

Quintain: A type of five-line poetry with perhaps eight syllables in length

Sari: A South Asian garment of a length of fabric draped around the body

Moringa: A subtropical tree bearing drumsticks containing high levels of antioxidant and anti-inflammatory compounds

CREDITS TO ARTISTS

All paintings showcased in this book of poetry are originals given by talented artists with their consent and courtesy.

Several ladies are professional artists with collections that they have exhibited, in various parts of the world; whilst a few are aspiring artisans.

I would like to thank each and every one of you for being part of my labour of love.

I would like to thank:

• Afshan Quraishy - India
• Graciela Ghirardosi - Argentina
• Kusum Dutta - India
• Majo Portilla - Netherlands
• Minisha Bhardwaj - India
• Seren Khalaf - Syria
• Sneh Mehta - UK
• Sonal Purohit - India
• Sumaira Isaacs - Pakistan
• Zaahirah Muthy - Mauritius

Your contribution in this book has made the poems more meaningful.

Thank you

A Parallel World

ABOUT THE AUTHOR

A Kenyan born girl, brought up in the UK and now residing in UAE, Roxana has spent her entire life chasing storms, and in the process has gathered many credits to her name. An Accountant by profession, she has an MBA from University of Liverpool in Leadership and is an alumni of the Harvard Business School. Passion and dreams sit on her shoulder as she leads with heart and strives to make the world a better place. She is the founder of the NGO – 'abc: an Advent for Building human Capital' (www.myabcfoundation.org) that accords skills to the unemployed in Hunza and Delhi to help them find financial sustenance, resulting in a 70% impact in growth. Her creativity outpours in her expression of spirituality through poetry she pens and the art she collects.

www.ingramcontent.com/pod-product-compliance
Lightning Source LLC
LaVergne TN
LVHW010032070426
835508LV00005B/300